Christianity

Early British Christianity, History of Christianity in England, Origin of Christianity.

Author
Kristos Howard

Copyright Notice

Copyright © 2017 Global Print Digital
All Rights Reserved

Digital Management Copyright Notice. This Title is not in public domain, it is copyrighted to the original author, and being published by **Global Print Digital**. No other means of reproducing this title is accepted, and none of its content is editable, neither right to commercialize it is accepted, except with the consent of the author or authorized distributor. You must purchase this Title from a vendor who's right is given to sell it, other sources of purchase are not accepted, and accountable for an action against. We are happy that you understood, and being guided by these terms as you proceed. Thank you

First Printing: 2017.

ISBN: 978-1-912483-40-2

Publisher: Global Print Digital.
Arlington Row, Bibury, Cirencester GL7 5ND
Gloucester
United Kingdom.
Website: www.homeworkoffer.com

Table of Content

Introduction 1
History of Christianity in England **18**
    Christianity in Roman Britain, ... 18
    Christianity in Anglo Saxon England 20
    Christianity in England in the Middle Ages 24
    Christianity in 16th Century England 27
    Christianity in 17th Century England 33
    Christianity in 18th Century England 37
Origin of Christianity **42**
    Origins 42
    The Bible and the Fundemental Rules of Christianity 45
    The Spread of Christianity to the Romans and by the Romans 51
    Christianity comes to England 56
    Power Struggles between Church and King 60
    The Start of a Religious Revolution 68
    The Reformation 73
    The Enlightenment 88
    Christianity in England Today 102
Early British Christianity **104**

Introduction

Christianity: The Religion of the Fatherhood of God and the Brotherhood of Man Mediated by Jesus Christ

Christianity, stemming out of Judaism and developing primarily in the West, has become the largest religion of the world even though, except for Islam, it is the youngest major world religion. Approximately one in every three persons on earth is identified with Christianity.

A religion practiced by so many people naturally encompasses a wide variety of beliefs and practices. In general Christians share a common belief in the uniqueness of Jesus of Nazareth as a truly divine and truly human incarnate Son of God who is the savior of mankind. They believe each individual by their faith and life determine their eternal destiny--either in heaven or in hell.

Scholars believe that Jesus, the founder of Christianity, was born between 4 and 7 B. C. at Bethlehem and grew up in Nazareth of Galilee. His contemporaries regarded him as the eldest son of Joseph, a carpenter, and his wife, Mary; but Matthew and Luke report that Jesus was born of a virgin. He grew up in a family of at least six other children. Roman Catholics maintain these were children of Joseph by an earlier marriage.

Since Jesus' parents were common people, it is assumed he attended the local synagogue school and was trained as a carpenter. The story of his discussion with the teachers of the law in Jerusalem when he was twelve suggests that he had an unusual interest and knowledge in religious matters. The next eighteen years are often called the silent years. Since Joseph drops out of the records at this point, it is assumed that he died during this period and that Jesus took over the management of the carpenter business along with the help of his brothers.

When Jesus was about thirty he began his ministry. The first public act was his baptism by his cousin, John the Baptist, in the Jordan river. Following his baptism, Jesus spent forty days in the Judean wilderness pondering the nature of his ministry. When he returned Jesus selected twelve apostles and spent three years preaching and teaching in Galilee, Judea, and Perea. His ministry was a balanced portrayal of the nature of God and service to man. Many were benefited by his miracles of healing. Peter described his life succinctly: "He went about doing good."

Both the form and content of Jesus' teachings are recognized and respected as outstanding among the great religious pioneers and innovators of the world. Jesus believed he was sent by God and accepted Peter's description of him as "the Christ" (Messiah). The basic teaching of Jesus was the love of God and the love of man. The fatherhood of God and the brotherhood of man is the essence of his gospel. This fellowship of the sons and daughters of God with each other and with their Heavenly Father Jesus referred to as the Kingdom of God or the Kingdom of Heaven.

We see in his life and teachings the centrality of the religious point of view. His primary concern was that he and all mankind should be completely dedicated to doing the will of God. Jesus saw the Kingdom of God as a progressive growth of the individual and society--a mustard seed phenomenon. Jesus emphasized the worth of human personality. Evil was to be opposed with vigor but persons must be loved unendingly. Ethically Jesus taught principles rather than rules.

Christianity

The spirit, the motivation, is the heart of behavior; external action or appearances are secondary. He saw body, mind, and spirit as a functional whole which is essentially good and capable of growth and improvement, striving toward the perfection of the Heavenly Father. Much of Jesus' most profound teaching is given in parables. Through his life and teachings he achieved a new synthesis of religious insights which has attracted people of all religions and has resulted in more books being written about him than about any person who has ever lived on our planet.

The leaders of Judaism increasingly threatened by his appeal to the common people and by his unorthodox teaching and behavior contrived to have him condemned by the Jewish high court and with the co-operation of the Roman Procurator of Judea, Pontius Pilate, had him crucified. The third day following his death the Gospels report his resurrection and after forty days, in which Jesus appeared to various groups of disciples, he ascended into heaven.

At Pentecost (Shavout, fifty days after Passover) his followers in Jerusalem experienced being filled with the Holy Spirit and they began preaching the gospel of their risen Lord with great enthusiasm and dedication. Peter and James assumed leadership of the Jerusalem Church until its destruction along with the city in 70 A.D.

Paul of Tarsus is often called "the second founder of Christianity." He was a Jewish scholar convert who is traditionally considered to be the author of fourteen books of the New Testament. Paul was the first to state systematically the beliefs of Christianity and is largely responsible for transforming a sect of Judaism into the early Christian Church where gentiles were welcome. John B. Noss says, "He brought intact the religion of Jesus in the vehicle of a religion about Jesus."

The Bible, made up of the Old Testament and the New Testament, is the scripture of Christianity. The New Testament began in the early Christian Church as a series of papers and letters written by numerous people. Over the years there was much discussion about which books should be officially recognized. In 367 Athanasius, Bishop of Alexandria, in an Easter letter discusses the books he considered canonical. This is the first list which includes all of the twenty-seven books in the New Testament as we now have it. Various church councils in the years that followed adopted this list.

The early Christian Church was not a highly organized body with an established creed; therefore, it encompassed a wide variety of beliefs. The most famous heresy of the early church centered around a widespread and diverse group known as Gnostics. They believed the spirit was good and that flesh was evil. Consequently, they denied that Christ could have been truly human. Jesus was not really born of the flesh and there was no resurrection of the flesh. The Gnostics also regarded Jehovah as an inferior being and rejected the Old Testament. Gnosticism was a syncretistic movement which incorporated beliefs of many Middle East religions and philosophies.

Marcionism was a closely related heresy. Marcion, the son of the Bishop of Pontus, declared that the God of the Old Testament was a cruelly legalistic and merciless deity and that Christians should discard the Old Testament and follow Paul in asceticism, celibacy, and scorn the physical world.

A third heresy, Montanism, was a theology preached by Montanus in the middle of the second century. Montanus taught that the Holy Spirit was not to be stifled by dogma but should be free to move in the hearts of Christians, causing them to speak in tongues and engage in other charismatic activities. He taught that the end of the world was coming soon.

To counter these and other heretical groups Irenaeus, Bishop of Lyons, wrote against the Heresies around 185 A. D. Later the Apostles Creed was adopted and the New Testament was canonized in an attempt to control religious beliefs. Modern scholars are finding the struggle with these deviant groups was much more complex than official records show. At times political and economic factors may have been more important in determining actions than the theological issues.

Early Christians, in addition to being torn by internal problems, were persecuted in the Roman empire. They were accused of being atheists who committed sexual atrocities and engaged in cannibalism. In such an environment gradually the Bishop of Rome for a variety of social, political, and ecclesiastical reasons came to be recognized as the most important bishop of

Christendom and was finally designated Pope. The Emperor Constantine whose wife and mother were Christians brought persecution to a close. In 325 he called the Church Council of Nicea to stop the warring within Christianity over the nature of Christ. Just before dying Constantine accepted baptism and officially became a Christian.

The writings of St. Augustine (354-430) formulating the doctrines of original sin, the fall of man, and predestination along with the rise of the monastic movement had a great influence on Christianity. Theological differences and deteriorating relationships between East and West finally resulted in a complete break in 1054 when the pope excommunicated the patriarch of Constantinople and precipitated the formation of the Eastern Orthodox Church.

The medieval papacy developed power, gathered lands, wealth, and went to war like any other feudal fiefdom. The moral leadership of the papacy was at its lowest ebb between 1309 and 1377. It was a time of luxury, moral laxity, and abuse. The papacy was moved from Rome to Avignon. In 1378 the Avignon cardinals elected a new pope, Urban VI, who refused to return to Avignon. The cardinals declared Urban's election void and elected another pope to rule from Avignon. Urban retaliated by selecting another college of cardinals who were stationed at Rome. The Council of Pisa called in 1409 to settle the issue resulted instead in electing a third pope who also claimed to be Christ's vicar on earth. The Great Schism was finally resolved at the Council of Constance which met from 1414 to 1418. Thomas Aquinas (1227-1274), a Dominican monk, who lived in this medieval historical period was one of the greatest thinkers the church ever produced. In his Summa Theologiae he applied Aristotelian philosophy to the formation of Christian theology in an attempt to bring faith and reason together.

The Renaissance, the rise of European nationalism, and the decline of the papacy set the stage for the Protestant Reformation. Forerunners like John Wyclif in England, John Huss in Bohemia, and Girolamo Savonarola in Italy helped prepare Europe for the Reformation initiated by Martin Luther when he nailed ninety-five theses on the door of the Wittenberg Church as grounds for debate. Ulrich Zwingli and John Calvin in Switzerland and John Knox in Scotland were the originators of the Reformed-Presbyterian churches. The marital problems of Henry VIII were instrumental in founding the Church of England, establishing the heritage of the Episcopal Church, and later the Methodist Church under the leadership of John and Charles Wesley.

The most radical of the Protestant groups were the Anabaptists in Switzerland and the Netherlands. They attempted to discard everything that was not expressly found in the New Testament. These nonconformists laid the foundation for the emergence of the Mennonites, Amish, Quakers, Congregationalists, Baptists, and Unitarians. Later social concerns resulted in the advent of the Salvation Army, the Young Men's Christian Association, and the Sunday School movement.

The Roman Catholic Counter-Reformation at the Council of Trent in 1545 declared that Catholic tradition was co-equal with scripture as a source of truth; and that the Roman Catholic Church had the sole right to interpret scripture. They reaffirmed the seven sacraments: Baptism, Confirmation, Penance, Eucharist, Extreme Unction, Marriage, and Ordination. (The Protestant churches recognize only Baptism and the Lord's Supper as sacraments.) Later the Catholic Church established the doctrines of the Immaculate Conception of Mary (1854) and the bodily assumption of Mary (1950).

The Vatican Council of 1869 declared the dogma of papal infallibility when the pope speaks ex cathedra. The Second Vatican Council called by John XXIII in 1958 and at meetings between 1962 and 1965 effected the most sweeping changes ever made in the Roman Catholic Church. It recognized Non-Catholics as true Christians; allowed the vernacular in the mass and more congregational participation in worship; declared Jews were not responsible for the death of Jesus; and took steps toward reconciliation with Orthodox and Protestant groups.

The nineteenth century was characterized by a strong missionary movement; and the twentieth century has given birth to the ecumenical movement. Churches all over the world are beginning to initiate fellowship and unite. The World Council of Churches was organized in Amsterdam in 1948. Denominations like the United Church of Christ, the United Methodist Church, and the United Presbyterian Church illustrate this trend.

With the rise of modern science and the ecumenical movement the mainline churches of Christianity became less doctrinaire and began utilizing scientific knowledge in their religious views. Many accepted evolution as the methodology which God used in creation and had no trouble with the possibility that there may be millions of inhabited planets in the universe.

There was a sharp reaction to this "modernism" by conservative churchmen who became known as fundamentalists. They denounced the National Council of Churches, evolution, and "worldliness." Fundamentalism stressed the infallibility and inerrancy of the Bible; the deity and virgin birth of Christ; the necessity of the substitutionary blood atonement doctrine; the physical or bodily resurrection of Christ; and the bodily second coming of Christ. These churches now prefer to be called "evangelicals." They have become quite militant in their evangelism and have a much larger missionary program than the mainline churches.

On the other extreme, liberal Christianity believes that Christianity is a dynamic and growing religion; that revelation is progressive and continuous; that God is personal and each person's religious experience in unique; that emphasis should be placed on man's inherent worth, dignity, and potentials as a child of God; and that the struggle against evil is both personal and social. Christianity must be thought out, deeply experienced, and lived in all of life.

John Noss sums up Christianity by saying, "Christianity is not a way of looking into the past, but a way of going forward into the future; not an escape from the world into solitariness, but a way of spending one's life in order to find it; not a retreat into ultimate truth, but a redemptive mission, a way of salvation leading into the world and through the world, in the love of God and man.

History of Christianity in England

Christianity in Roman Britain,

The first evidence of Christianity in what is now England is from the late 2nd century AD. (There may have been Christians in Britain before then, we cannot be sure). Roman Britain was a cosmopolitan place. Merchants from all over the empire settled there and soldiers from many countries served there so we will never know who first introduced Christianity to Britain.

At that time the native people were Celts. They were polytheists (they worshiped many gods). The Romans too were polytheists and they were willing to allow the Celts to worship their old gods.

However, the Romans were not tolerant of Christianity. At times waves of persecution crossed the empire. St Alban the first British Christian martyr was executed in a town called Verulamium in 304 AD. Much later an abbey was built there dedicated to St Alban and it gave its name to the town of St Albans.

In 313 the Emperor Constantine granted Christians freedom of worship. So persecution ended and during the 4th century Christianity became widespread in England.

In 314 three British bishops attended a church council in Arles in France, Eborius bishop of York, Restitutus bishop of London and Adelius bishop of Caerleon (Gwent). So by that time there was a flourishing and organised church in England.

In Hinton St Mary, Dorset a 4th century mosaic was found with the face of Jesus and the Greek letters chi rho, which stand for christos (Greek for Christ) showing Christianity was a popular religion in England.

Christianity in Anglo Saxon England

In 407 the last Roman soldiers left Britain. Over the following decades Roman civilization broke down. In the 5th and 6th centuries Pagan peoples the Saxons, Angles and Jutes from Germany and Denmark invaded southern and eastern England and gradually conquered most of England.

However Christianity continued to thrive in Wales and by the early 5th century it spread to Ireland. In the 5th and 6th centuries Scotland was converted. Cut off from the Church in Rome Celtic Christians formed a distinctive Celtic Church.

Christianity

According to tradition Pope Gregory saw boys on sale in the slave market in Rome. He is supposed to have asked about them and when told that they were Angles he replied 'not Angles but angels' When he became Pope he was keen to convert the Anglo-Saxons. In 596 he sent a party of about 40 men led by Augustine to Kent. They arrived in 597.

Aethelberht permitted the monks to preach in Kent and in time he was converted. (The king of Kent was married to a Christian princess named Berta. It may have been partly due to her influence that Kent was converted to Christianity). Furthermore, his nephew, Saeberht, the king of Essex was also converted.

Meanwhile in 627 King Edwin of Northumbria (in the North of England) and all his nobles were baptized. (He may have been influenced by his wife, Ethelburgh, who was a Christian). Most of his subjects followed.

However, things did not go smoothly in Northumbria. King Edwin was killed at the battle of Hatfield in 632 and afterwards most of Northumbria reverted to Paganism. They had to be converted all over again by Celtic monks from Scotland.

Further south in 630 a Christian called Sigeberht became King of East Anglia. He asked the Archbishop of Canterbury to send men to help convert his people. Meanwhile Pope Honorious sent a man named Birinus to convert the West Saxons (who lived in Hampshire).

Missionaries also preached in the kingdom of Mercia (The Midlands). In 653 King Paeda of Mercia was converted and baptized and gradually the realm was converted. The last part of England to be converted to Christianity was Sussex. It was converted after 680 by St. Wilfrid.

Finally, by the end of the 7th century all of England was at least nominally Christian. However, some people continued to secretly worship the old pagan gods as late as the 8th century.

However, in the late 9th century the Danes conquered most of England. However, in 878 Alfred the Great, king of Wessex (Southern England) crushed the Danes at the battle of Edington. Afterwards the Danes made a treaty with Alfred. They split England between them. The Danes took all the territory east of the old Roman road, Watling Street. The Danes also agreed to become Christians.

Once they were converted to Christianity the Danes of Eastern England had much in common with the Saxons. Gradually Alfred's descendants conquered the Danish-held areas of England and in time they created a single kingdom of England.

Then in the late 10th century there was a religious revival. A man named Dunstan (c.1020-1088) was Archbishop of Canterbury. He reformed the monasteries. Many new churches and monasteries were built during his time. Women played a significant part in the 10th century revival.

Christianity in England in the Middle Ages

In the Middle Ages religion was a vital part of everyday life. All children were baptized (unless they were Jewish) and everyone attended mass on Sunday. Mass was in Latin, a language that ordinary people did not understand.

Bishops ruled over groups of parishes called dioceses. They usually came from rich families. Bishops lived in palaces and often took part in government. Things were very different for parish priests. They were poor and often had little education. Parish priests had their own land called the glebe where they grew their own food. They lived and worked alongside their parishioners.

In the Middle Ages monks and nuns gave food to the poor. They also ran the only hospitals where they tried to help the sick as best they could. They also provided hospitality for pilgrims and other travelers (although as time went by there were an increasing number of inns where you could pay to stay the night). In a medieval monastery there was an almonry where food or money was given to the poor, the refectory where the monks ate, the dormitory, infirmary and the cloisters where the monks could take exercise. An almoner looked after the poor, an infirmarian looked after the sick and a hospitaller looked after visitors.

As well as the monks from the 13th century there were also friars. They took vows like but instead of withdrawing from the world they went out to preach. Franciscan friars were called grey friars because of their grey costumes. Dominican friars were called black friars.

In the Middle Ages merchants and groups of craftsmen were organised into guilds, which protected their interests. Guilds also put on plays called mystery play. (The word mystery is a corruption of the French word metier, meaning job or trade). The plays were based on Bible stories and were meant to instruct the people. However, there was nothing solemn about these plays. They contained lots of jokes.

In the 14th and 15th centuries the Virgin Mary and the saints were given much more prominence in religion. Far more devotion was shown to them. Furthermore, rich people paid for chantries, which were chapels where a priest said prayers for the dead in the belief that they would shorten the period the dead person would spend suffering in purgatory before they could enter Heaven. Some people bought indulgences (certificates which, they believed would shorten the time they had to spend in purgatory.

A famous Christian of the 14th century was John Wycliffe. He denied the doctrine of transubstantiation (the belief that bread and wine are transformed into the body and blood of Christ during mass). His followers translated the Bible into English. Wycliffe died of natural causes but his followers were persecuted. They were known as Lollards (a word that meant mutterers) because they said long prayers. In 1401 a law was passed which allowed heretics to be burned to death. Nevertheless, the Lollards continued to meet during the 15th century.

Christianity in 16th Century England

One of the great Christians of the early 16th century was William Tyndale. In 1525 Tyndale translated the

New Testament into English. Tyndale also translated part of the Old Testament. However, Tyndale was burned in 1536. His last words were 'Lord open the king of England's eyes'. Meanwhile Protestant ideas were spreading in England despite persecution by the state.

In 1501 Arthur the oldest son of King Henry VII married Catherine of Aragon. However, Arthur died in 1502. His brother Henry now became heir to the throne. He married his brother's widow in 1509. (Normally such a marriage would not have been allowed but the Pope gave a special dispensation).

At the beginning of 1511 Henry VIII had a son but the boy died after only 7 weeks. Catherine had four miscarriages and only one of her children lived - a girl named Mary. Henry was desperate to have a son and heir and Catherine could not give him one.

Henry decided that God was punishing him for marrying his brother's widow. Henry now argued that the marriage to Catherine was not valid and he asked the Pope to annul the marriage. However, the Pope would not co-operate.

The Henrician Reformation

Finally, Henry lost patience with the Pope and rejected his authority in 1534. The Act of Supremacy made Henry the head of the Church of England. However, although Henry broke with Rome he kept the Catholic religion essentially intact in England. Henry had no intention of changing the English religion to Lutheranism and he continued to persecute Protestants. In 1539 Henry VIII passed the Act of Six Articles, which laid down the beliefs of the Church of England. The Six Articles preserved the old religion mainly intact. However, in 1539 Henry authorized a new new English translation of the Bible and from 1545

English replaced Latin as the language of church services.

Meanwhile Henry dissolved the monasteries in England. Parliament agreed to dissolve the small ones in 1536. The large ones followed in 1539-1540.

Shortly before Henry VIII died a woman named Anne Askew was martyred. Anne was a preacher and teacher. However, in 1546 she was arrested, tortured in the Tower of London and burned.

Edward VI

Henry finally died in 1547 and he was succeeded by his 9-year-old son Edward. Since he was too young to rule his uncle, Edward Seymour, Duke of Somerset, was made protector and ruled in his stead.

Somerset was a devout Protestant as was Archbishop Cranmer. They began to turn England into a truly Protestant country. The Act of Six Articles was repealed and in 1549 the first Book of Common Prayer, the first Anglican prayer book was issued. Meanwhile priests were allowed to marry and pictures or statues of Mary or the saints were removed from churches. In 1552 a second prayer book was issued. Also in Edward's reign the chantries (where a priest prayed for the souls of the dead) were closed.

Mary

In 1553 Edward died and he was followed by his sister Mary. She was a Catholic and she detested the changes of Henry VIII and Edward VI. Mary was determined to undo the reforms of the two previous reigns. Catholic mass was restored in December 1553. In 1554 married clergy were ordered to leave their wives or lose their posts. Then, in November 1554 the Act of Supremacy was repealed.

In 1555 Mary began burning Protestants. Over the next 3 years nearly 300 Protestants were executed. Many more Protestants fled abroad. However, Mary's cruelty simply gained sympathy for the Protestants and alienated ordinary people. She simply drove people away from Roman Catholicism.

Elizabeth I

Elizabeth I was crowned in January 1559. She restored Protestantism to England. The Act of Supremacy was restored in April 1559 and further Acts replaced Catholic practices. However, it was a moderate Protestantism. Elizabeth disliked extremists. She disapproved of the Puritans. (They were people who wanted to 'purify' the Church of England of its remaining Catholic elements).

However most of the population (not all) accepted the religious settlement. People could be fined for not attending church. Nevertheless, some Catholics continued to practice their religion in secret.

Meanwhile clergymen became better educated during the 16th century. By the end of the century many of them did a degree.

Christianity in 17th Century England

In the early 17th century king and parliament clashed over the issue of religion. In 1633 William Laud was made Archbishop of Canterbury. He was strongly opposed to the Puritans and King Charles I supported him wholeheartedly. Laud emphasized the ceremony and decoration in churches. These measures were strongly opposed by the Puritans. They feared it was the 'thin edge of the wedge' and Catholicism would eventually be restored in England.

Meanwhile in the 16th century everybody was supposed to belong to the Church of England. However, in the 17th century independent churches were formed. The first Baptist Church in England began meeting in 1612.

Later in the 17th century George Fox (1624-1691) and Margaret Fell (1614-1702) founded the Quakers. Fox believed that everybody had an inner light and during the 1660s and the 1670s he traveled across England. Margaret Fell wrote a book called Women's Speaking Justified, Proved and Knowed of the Scriptures. However, the Quakers were persecuted and Fox himself was often imprisoned.

From the end of the 16th century there were also Congregationalists or Independents. They believed that every congregation had a right to run its own affairs without any outside interference.

In 1642 came Civil War between king and parliament. It ended in 1646 and Charles I was executed in 1649. Following the Civil War and the execution of the king many independent churches sprang up in England.

Charles II became king in 1660. The king was not particularly religious but parliament was determined to crack down on the many independent churches that had sprung up and make Anglicanism the state religion again. They passed a series of acts called the Clarendon code, a series of laws to persecute non-conformists (Protestants who did not belong to the Church of England). The Corporation Act of 1661 said that all officials in towns must be members of the Church of England.

The Act of Uniformity 1662 said that all clergy must use the Book of Common Prayer. About 2,000 clergy who disagreed resigned. Furthermore, the Conventicle Act of 1664 forbade unauthorized religious meetings of more than 5 people unless they were all of the same household.

Finally, the Five Mile Act of 1665 forbade non-Anglican ministers to come within 5 miles of incorporated towns. (Towns with a mayor and corporation). However, these measures did not stop the non-conformists meeting or preaching.

When Charles II died in 1685 he was followed by James II, who was openly Catholic. James II promptly alienated the people by appointing Catholics to powerful and important positions. In 1687 he went further and issued a Declaration of Indulgence suspending all laws against Catholics and Protestant non-Anglicans.

James II was deposed in 1688. Afterwards the Bill of Rights (1689) said that no Catholic could become king or queen and no king could marry a Catholic. Parliament also passed the Toleration Act in 1689. Non-conformists were allowed their own places of worship and their own teachers and preachers. However, they could not hold government positions or attend university.

Christianity in 18th Century England

In the early 18th century England was noted for its lack of religious enthusiasm. It was an age of reason rather than dogmatism and the churches lacked vigor. However, in the mid-18th century things began to change. In 1739 the great evangelist George Whitefield (1714-1770) began preaching. Also in 1739 John Wesley (1703-1791) began preaching. He eventually created a new religious movement called the Methodists.

John Wesley traveled all over the country, often preaching in open spaces. People jeered at his meetings and threw stones but Wesley persevered. John Wesley never intended to form a movement separate from the Church of England. However, the Methodists did eventually break away.

At the end of the 18th century a group of Evangelical Christians called the Clapham Sect were formed. They campaigned for an end to slavery and cruel sports. They were later called the Clapham Sect because so many of them lived in Clapham. Meanwhile in the late 18th century religious enthusiasm began to revive in England.

Christianity in 19th Century England

During the 19th century Britain was transformed by the industrial revolution. In 1801, at the time of the first census, only about 20% of the population lived in towns. By 1851 the figure had risen to over 50%. By 1881 about two thirds of the population lived in towns.

During the early 19th century religious revival continued. The Church of England regained its energy and many new churches were built.

Meanwhile in 1829 the Catholic Emancipation Act was passed. Since the Reformation Catholics had been unable to become MPs or to hold public office. The Act restored those rights to them.

Organised religion was much more important in 19th century England than it is today. Nevertheless, in 1851 a survey showed that only about 40% of the population were at church or chapel on a given Sunday. Even allowing for those who were ill or could not make it for some other reason it meant that half the population did not go to church. Certainly many of the poor had little or no contact with the church. In 1881 a similar survey showed only about 1/3 of the population at church on a given Sunday. In the late 19th century organised religion was in decline in England.

During the 19th century many poor workers had little or no contact with the church. In 1865 William and Catherine Booth founded a new movement to reach the poor and fight a 'war' against poverty. In 1878 it was named the Salvation Army.

Christianity in 20th Century England

During the 20th century church going declined rapidly in England and by the end of the 20th century only a small minority of the population attended church regularly. Nevertheless most people continued to believe in God and in the late 20th century there was a hunger for the spiritual. There was an explosion of interest in the occult and the New Age Movement.

Meanwhile in the early 20th century Pentecostal churches were formed. They practiced the gifts of the Holy Spirit such as praying in tongues. In the 1960s use of the gifts of the Holy Spirit spread to mainstream churches. In the 1970s and 1980s charismatic or 'house churches' became common. At the end of the 20th century the Alpha Course became an effective method of introducing people to Christianity.

Christianity

Origin of Christianity
Origins

Christianity, now 2000 years old was originally intended to be a modification to Judaism (The religion of the Jews going back more than 2500 years). The founder, Jesus, a man born a Jew in modern day Israel, thought the Jewish religion was flawed and needed bringing up to date. He had many religious and moral points to make which made him very unpopular with both the Jews and the Romans of the day, which included:

- ✓ The Jewish faith was only available to those born a Jew. Hence was a divisive religion.

Christianity

- ✓ A religious faith should be open to all.
- ✓ The Jewish faith did not concentrate sufficiently on the poor. That is attention needed to be directed to those in need. Also it is easier to be a good poor man than a good rich man.
- ✓ The Jewish view of an eye for an eye and a tooth for a tooth was barbaric. Jesus preached a very tough alternative, "turn the other cheek". Clearly a suggestion that a discussion might avert a war.

Jesus also preached forgiveness. This has been interpreted by the Roman Church as forgiveness through confession. That is if you confess to a priest, God will not hold your sin against you when its your time to die and go to paradise (Heaven). The priest is not in any circumstances obliged to tell the police even in the case of murder. (Roman Catholics only)

Original Texts And Scriptures.

Jesus as with many other prophets did not write down his own set of instructions and left it instead to others. In the case of Jesus his immediate followers provided a record of what Jesus taught but written from memory more than 50 years after his death in the form of easy to read and astonishing stories. The main contributors were Matthew, Mark, Luke and John plus the prolific letter writer and evangelist, the gentile (or non Jew) Paul.

The three most important written instructions for Christians are:

1. The Bible, Old Testament. The first five books of which are also followed by Jews.

2. Bible, New Testament, where the words written by Matthew and Mark etc are recorded.

3. The Crede, written by Roman Christians about 1700 years ago in the monasteries around

Istanbul (Turkey), then Constantinople, the then capital of the Eastern Roman empire of Byzantium.

As with some other religions the interpretation of the written words must be by ordinary mortals who are prone to disagree particularly as their first language is not necessarily the language of the original scribe. In addition the interpretations need to be continuously brought up to date for example as required by science (example birth control and genetic engineering) and social customs (example the role of women). Therein lie further problems which have regularly created splits (schisms) in the church and new cults or denominations.

The Bible and the Fundemental Rules of Christianity

The most important parts of the Bible for Christians are:

Firstly -The Ten Commandments

The Ten Commandments are shared between the Jews and the Christians. These rules for life were thought by Moses to be given to him by God on Mount Sinai in the now Egyptian Sinai desert when he (Moses) was leading the Israelites out of slavery in Egypt en route to the "Promised Land" which is present day Israel plus the Palestinian West Bank. (About 2500 years ago). They are: (Bible, Exodus Ch. 20)

- ✓ Honour your father and mother
- ✓ Don't kill other humans
- ✓ Do not commit adultery
- ✓ Do not envy or long to own your neighbours house, or wife, nor anything that belongs to your neighbour
- ✓ Do not tell lies about your neighbour

Christianity

- ✓ Do not steal
- ✓ Work for six days a week
- ✓ On the seventh rest but this is also Gods day.
- ✓ Do not mention God's name without reverence.
- ✓ Do not make models or icons about God or Heaven.

Jesus added to these some 500 years later on another desert mountain in what is now called the Sermon on the Mount as follows:

(Ref.: Bible New Testament, Matthew chapters 5/6/7)

- ✓ Blessed are the meek for they shall inherit the earth
- ✓ Blessed are the peacemakers for they shall be called the sons of God
- ✓ Blessed are the merciful for they will obtain mercy

- ✓ Blessed are the pure in heart for they shall see God
- ✓ Blessed are those who hunger and thirst after righteousness for they shall be satisfied.
- ✓ Blessed are those who are persecuted for righteousness sake for theirs is the kingdom of heaven.
- ✓ Blessed are the poor in spirit, for theirs is the kingdom of heaven
- ✓ Blessed are those who mourn for they shall be comforted

At the same time Jesus took the opportunity to strengthen the rules of the Ten Commandments for example he said:

- ✓ Remember what the old timers said about adultery, as far as I'm concerned you have committed adultery if you so much as think about sleeping with another man's wife.

- ✓ It was also said by the old timers, "If you divorce your wife give her a certificate (Testimonial letter)". I say if you divorce your wife for anything other than unchastity (refusing to have sex with you) makes her an adulteress and who ever marries a divorced woman commits adultery.
- ✓ Remember also the words "Thou shalt not kill." "I say to you every one who is angry, even with his friend, shall be liable for punishment."

What Jesus left out.

The Ten Commandments were ten out of more than one hundred given to Moses by God some 500 years before Jesus gave "his Sermon on the Mount." Here are a few examples of some Jesus left out:

(See Exodus chapter 20/1/2/3 for the complete list.)

- ✓ If a man has sex with a maiden (virgin) he must marry her. (Ch. 22 v.16)
- ✓ If her father refuses, he shall give the virgin's father a suitable present (dowry) and then marry her. (Ch 22 v. 17)
- ✓ If a man has sex with an animal he must be put to death (Ch 22 v.19)
- ✓ If a man takes an additional wife she must in no way be treated worse than the first. (Ch 21 v 10)
- ✓ If a man kills another man he must be put to death. (Ch 21 v 12)
- ✓ If a man hits his Father or his Mother he must be put to death

Secondly - Prayer

At the same time Jesus told his followers that it was important that they should pray regularly. He also advised that private prayer (e.g. at home) would be more valuable than public prayer (e.g. in the street).

Christianity

The basic prayer he gave at this time was. (Freely translated)

Our Father who is in heaven,

Glorious is your name,

Your kingdom will come,

Your rules will be obeyed,

On this Earth as they are in Heaven.

Please give us this day the food we need.

Please also forgive us our sins,

As we have been told to forgive those who sin against us.

Please also lead us away from temptation and evil.

Thank you God,

For ever and ever

Amen

The Spread of Christianity to the Romans and by the Romans

2000 years ago

The next phase of the story of Christianity is the conversion of some Romans from their pagan faiths to Christianity. The man responsible around AD 50 was the non Jewish travelling evangelist, the Pharisee Paul. The Romans like the Greeks before them were wealthy enough to have time on their hands to think. Indeed Roman scholars took many of the thoughts of the Greek philosophers (Inc. Socrates and Aristotle) to fine tune the stories and teachings of Jesus.

The message of the early Christians was so strong that inspite of Roman resistance and in many places local persecution, within 100 years there were centres of Christianity throughout the Roman Empire, even in the far outposts of Roman Britain. A good example though a little later is from present day St Albans (20 miles north of London England): a priest was fleeing a lynching mob and was hidden by an early local

Christian in the then Roman town of Verulamium. When confronted by the mob (AD 304) saying "have you seen a priest?" said he was the priest and was immediately killed. St Alban as he is now known was the first known English martyr. A huge abbey marks the spot where the murder took place

The breakthrough came with the conversion of the Roman Emperor Constantine in AD 312 who set about making Christianity the official religion of the Roman Empire. Things moved quickly. Constantine changed the name of the eastern capital of the Roman Empire from Byzantium to Constantinople (After himself) and set up important religious colleges in the attractive local countryside. One by the lake called Nicaea. (Now in Turkey and called Iznik some 100 miles south east of Istanbul). From this college, the Roman Christian religious clerics produced a written document (in 325 AD) stating what Christians should believe. (It is now called the Nicaean Creed. The Latin for "I believe" is "Credo"). It is still used today as follows:

THE NICAEAN CREED

"I believe in one God the Father Almighty, Maker of heaven and earth, And of all things visible and invisible: And in one Lord Jesus Christ, the only begotten son of God, Begotten of his Father before all worlds, God of God Light of Light, Very God of very God, Begotten not made, Being of one substance with the Father, By whom all things were made.

Who for us men, and for our salvation came down from Heaven, And was incarnate by the Holy Ghost of the Virgin Mary, And was made man, And was crucified by Pontius Pilot, He suffered and was buried, And on the third day he rose again according to the scriptures, And ascended into Heaven, And sitteth on the right hand of the Father. And he will come again with glory to judge both the quick and the dead: Whose kingdom shall have no end.

And I believe in the Holy Ghost the Lord giver of life, Who proceedeth from the father and the Son, Who with the father and the Son together is worshiped and glorified, Who spake by the prophets. And I believe in one Catholic and Apostolic Church. I acknowledge one baptism for the remission of sins. And I look for the Resurrection of the dead and the life of the world to come". Amen

This creed lasted with very little competition for over 1000 years that is until the Reformation (circa AD 1500). However in the hundred or so years before it was agreed, the Christian church welcomed debate and intellectual speculation. The opposite would be the case as the Roman Popes fostered theological conformity. Particularly and not surprisingly, in the 2nd century there was much debate about the Holy Trinity

(God, Jesus and the Holy Spirit being one and the same thing.)

Saint Augustine of Hippo (354-430)
Some call him the father of the Christian church. Born in Thagaste close to the North African Roman town of Carthage (modern day Tunisia) he took a Christian wife and was finally converted to Christianity by the Roman Bishop of Milan St Ambrose. As Bishop of Hippo (300 miles west of Carthage in present day Algeria) he wrote the most influential books on Christianity for more than 800 years. Of particular interest and importance to the English was his influence on the Roman Britain St Patrick who became the patron saint of Ireland who travelled to Hippo to learn from him.

Christianity comes to England
THE HOLY ROMAN EMPIRE. THE IRISH EFFECT. SAINT PATRICK. MONASTERIES.

Christianity

1500 years ago

The next milestone in the development of the Roman Christian church came in 590AD though the powerful dogma of Pope Gregory 1st More than anybody he was responsible for removing any government control over the Church. (He had to come to an agreement with the ruling race in northern Italy at the time, the Lombards of Milan, one of the Germanic tribes who assisted in the fall of the Roman Empire)

Pope Gregory sponsored his emissary Augustine to fully convert England, then ruled by the Saxons, to Christianity. This was the first organised plan to spread Christianity to England. Around the same time Irish missionaries (Columba 521-597) who had been converted to Christianity by the Irish St Patrick movement, landed on the west coast of Scotland. Both movements survived the vicious pagan Viking invasions into both England and Ireland between 800 and 1000

AD. The writings of the Venerable Bede (written around 700AD in a monastery in Jarrow in Northumberland founded by the St Patrick movement) are a testimonial to this.(e.g. his "Ecclesiastical History of the English People").

Three other major events took place in Europe to fully establish the Christian Church across Europe. The Roman Byzantium Empire centred in Constantinople was not over run by the Germanic tribes as befell Rome

Pope Leo 3rd in about 800 came to a deal with the effective Emperor of Europe, Charlemagne, and crowned him Emperor of the Western Church or Holy Roman Emperor. (Charlemagne was of German stock whose court was in Aachen/Aix-la-Chapelle in the west of Germany.) On Charlemagne's death the crown passed to the German Kings. The best remembered of course being the Habsburgs whose court was in Vienna

Austria and then perhaps Charles 5th from Burgundy now in France who also became king of Spain and Naples in Italy The succession of the Holy Roman Empire remained solid until 1800 when it collapsed under Napoleon.

Perhaps the most holy, respected and useful activities of the Christian church were their monasteries which were centres for dedicated religious people to live, work and pray, generally eight times a day. They became the best brains of their day and most importantly did good works in their neighbourhood. This took the form of creating books for reading before printing was invented, teaching, the only real source of education at the time, and such things as helping local farmers with capital projects they could not afford like draining the land.

The men and women who lived in monasteries took vows to spend their lives doing good works in the name of God. Marriage was disallowed for monks and nuns. The first simple monasteries were set up in Ireland by St Patrick where one of their key jobs was to make copies, by hand of course, of all the vital Christian books being rapidly destroyed by the Saxons and Vikings in England. The official founder of the movement was the Italian St Benedict who was not a priest but set up 12 monasteries manned by 12 monks each. Around 525 AD he and a few monks established a centre in Monte Cassino and set out the rules for monastic life which have not changed much to this day. A number of universities owe their origins to monasteries notably Paris 1100 and Oxford 1249. The Pope's emissary St Augustine founded the Benedictine monastery at Canterbury in 597 AD.

Power Struggles between Church and King

Plus, POWER STRUGGLES BETWEEN CHRISTIANS AND MUSLIMS

CRUSADES

THE CHRISTIAN CHURCH SPLITS BETWEEN ROME AND CONSTANTINOPLE.

1000 years ago

There were three main authorities "governing" England over the next 500 years:

- ✓ The King
- ✓ His Barons (eventually became a parliament after Magna Carta)
- ✓ And the Church

A power struggle waxed and waned between the three. The Church under the guidance of the Archbishop of Canterbury organised the daily life of the people. A massive church building programme gave each village a parish church. A monastery to help with major capital projects was never far away.

A good example of the power struggle between an English King and Roman Church is illustrated in the story of King Henry 2nd (1154-1189) and his friend and Archbishop Thomas Becket. Henry was one of the best kings England ever had and at the time was the best King in Europe. He ruled the whole of the British Isles including Ireland and more of France than the contemporary French King. Henry was noted for his efforts to improve justice for everybody, equally, regardless of power or rank.

To put things in perspective, it was customary at this time for justice to be metered out by the baron's men in the most barbaric ways. The suspect was proven guilty or innocent by immersing a bandaged hand into boiling water for some minutes. The man was innocent if when the bandages were taken off he had no blisters! Some men were exempt from this, most notably the Bishops. Their judgement was based on a test of eating bread at the trial. His peers were asked to pray to the angel Gabriel and ask him to make the priest choke if guilty. Not too many were found guilty! Henry wanted two things. The same rules for everybody and the judges to report to the King.

Things were brought to a head when a bishop was tried in the old way for murder. The King complained to his friend and Archbishop Becket. Becket maintained the church was exempt and not only this, the final adjudicator for a churchman was the Pope in Rome. The friendship between the two men evaporated and Becket fled to northern France. The King very much missed Becket who he had made his political right hand man (Chancellor) as well as Archbishop.

Finally Becket returned to Canterbury Cathedral but the arguments between these two highly intelligent men with different views persisted. By chance Henry was overheard by four Knights to say (perhaps in jest) "Why am I surrounded by such a load of dumb heads none of whom have the guts to rid me of this pestilent priest." The Knights immediately travelled to Canterbury and killed Becket in his cathedral (1170). Of course the King was devastated but the story illustrated a political and religious structure designed without a single line of authority and hence the time bomb set to explode some 300 years later. (See the Reformation)

The Start Of An 800 Year War With The Muslims

A little earlier, immediately after the turn of the millennium (and coincidentally?) just 40 years after the breakaway from Rome by the Church in Constantinople, 1054, see below) Pope Urban 2nd in Rome answered a call for help from Constantinople(1095) for military action against the Muslims who were threatening their territory. The

Pope thus called upon the kings across Europe to wage a holy war against the Muslims mainly to recapture the Christian (and Jewish) holy city of Jerusalem (Indeed the Muslims moved into Jerusalem very soon after the start of their movement. Circa 700 AD) . These crusades lasted on and off almost 500 years and in general were an expensive failure from a Christian point of view. The English Norman King, Richard the Lion Heart who inherited the throne from Henry 2nd in 1189 spent most of his ten year reign, not looking after his extensive empire in England and France but swanning about at the Popes behest in middle eastern crusades (holy wars). He had some success in the sense he retook Jerusalem, and also had the sense to talk to the great Muslim ruler of Egypt and Syria, the Turk Saladin. to get permanent access for Christian pilgrims into Jerusalem.

The First Major Split In The Christian Church

The formation of the Eastern Orthodox Christian Church

The Eastern Christian church in Constantinople split (1054) with the rest of the Church headquartered in Rome and formed the Orthodox Church. The dispute was both theological and political. After all Constantinople was the headquarters of the only remaining part of the proud old Roman Empire and they were unhappy about the dogmatic (theological) authority from Rome. They froze the rules preached by the church up to the Nicean Creed. They also permitted the inclusion of elaborate Icons and perhaps most importantly claimed the authority of the Apostolic succession hence claimed they were the only true church.

View the History of Orthodox Christianinty

The Islmic Enemy

The Muslim Arabs spread their faith across the whole

of North Africa and up into Southern and Eastern (Aragon) Spain. This created not only huge problems for the Christians in the North of Spain but also the rest of Europe. For some 500 years the Muslim Arabs and the Muslim Ottomans controlled the European sources and trade routes for Gold and Spices. Gold, required to make currency was running out in Europe. The Arabs had plenty, mined in North Africa at Gao close to Timbuktu in present day Mali. Spices (mainly pepper which the Romans thought was almost as valuable as Gold) came from Java, in present day Indonesia and came to Europe via the Arab trading port in Egypt of Alexandria. The Christian/Muslim wars lasted some 700 years were ended finally by the English at the height of their Naval and imperial powers of 200 years ago.

Christian And Jews

Christians, in this period also suffered the self inflicted

economic constraint as the Roman controlled Christian Church did not allow the setting up of financial institutions like banks as part of Christian religious laws. The Jewish faith permitted money lending (Usury). William the Conqueror (a Christian) asked the Jews in France to come to England with him to ensure this service was available in his new domain. England had to wait 500 years until Elizabeth 1st ruled as a Protestant Queen and money lending by Protestant Christians were allowed.

The Start of a Religious Revolution

750 years ago

The Christian Church is seen to become too powerful and too dogmatic

From 1000 years ago, with the economic and cultural stability brought to England by the Normans both Church and state flourished. The Church ran life at grass routes level which included the collection of religious taxes from the people. Probably more happily given than the state taxes collected by the Barons. Much of the Church money would have had to go to Rome. However the local Bishops seemed to be doing rather well perhaps some even living the high life. This caused resentment amongst the people most who lived just above starvation level if the harvest was poor.

One of the first to complain was Oxford University philosopher John Wycliffe (1329-1384). However being a University Don his complaint was mainly about theological issues. He wanted the church to get back to basics that the bible taught rather than the interpretation authorised by the Popes. A particular point was the doctrine of "Transubstantiation". That is the Roman Christian doctrine states that during Mass in Church, when the priest offers wine and bread as a symbol for Jesus' blood and body that they actually turn into the blood and body of Jesus. Wycliffe was kicked out of Oxford and labelled a heretic. His Fundamentalist thinking was carried forward by the Lollards.

The main issues were, Transubstantiation.

The rule that the Church in Rome could effectively interpret the Bible as it wished. Wycliffe thought individuals should interpret the bible as they wished.

He also attacked the hierarchy of the church. That is the power of Bishops etc.

All these points were adopted by the English Protestants 150 years later.

What Wycliffe complained about was mirrored across Europe by other independent but like minded observers.

Also during this period the English Kings had to balance their control of the country with the power of the Church of Rome sometimes providing different rules.

500 years ago

The Renaissance and the Reformation in the Christian Church

Three events elevated Europe from a medieval society to what we have now, as represented by freedom of thought, speech and writing and a respect of our fellow human beings or Human Rights. These movements started in Italy and spread rapidly through Europe then west to America with the European explorers and eventually, with the English to South Africa, Australia and New Zealand. (The areas dominated by the Islamic Ottomans were closed to Europeans and hence closed to Renaissance thinking.)

The three events were:

- ✓ The Cultural Renaissance
- ✓ Science
- ✓ The Religious Reformation

Without the first two the Reformation would not have happened.

Renaissance is a French word that means Re-birth. The Roman Christian church had ruled for 1000 years across the whole of Europe. The message was very appealing. If you follow the rules laid down by the Pope in Rome, when you die you will go to paradise (heaven). A very powerful promise when the length of life was so short. Of course the rules included the payment of religious taxes, mainly in the form of farm and property taxes as the Church owned so much land via both the Monasteries and the Church Parishes. The Church was the only source of education and scholarship. Indeed generally the only people who could read in the land were either the clergy or those few trained by the clergy. The penalty for arguing with the church (Heresy) was death.

The catalyst for this revolutionary thinking or re-birth

was the fall of the headquarters of the Eastern Christian church in Constantinople to the Muslim Ottomans in 1453 after some 250 years of military conflict. Whereas the German Vandals who sacked Rome some 1000 years earlier left nothing, this time many of the scholars and theologians in Constantinople who fled made it to northern Italy. They brought with them their ancient books describing not only the teachings of the Eastern Church but also the almost 2000 years of thoughts and art from the Greeks and Romans which had been lost to the western world. A freedom of thought, science and art was reborn.

The Reformation

The ideas of the early "reformers" were to change the "bad" or earthly habits that the Church of Rome had in their opinion fallen into. (Similar in a way to how Jesus had set out to Reform the "corrupt" Jewish Church). As with Jesus the early reformers were risking death by confronting the establishment. Without the fall of Constantinople it might never have happened. The first reformer is said to have been the German Monk, Martin Luther when in 1517 he nailed up his 95 complaints against the Church in Rome on the door of the castle church at Wittenburg

Following many trips to Rome, he failed to reform the church, and was immediately condemned to death by the Pope but with the support of some German princes he survived and formed the Protestant movement. He was followed in Switzerland by Zwingli (1520) and in France(actually Geneva in Switzerland) by the more extreme fundamentalist, Frenchman John Calvin. All these men of course were preceded by 150 years by Oxford English scholar John Wycliffe who had exactly the same ideas and complaints. Wycliffe and the Lollards did not have the weight of the Renaissance behind them. Also by the Italian Friar, Savonarola who was burnt at the stake in Florence in 1498.

Eventual country converts to the new Protestant thinking were:

- ✓ England 1552 after various blood baths.
- ✓ Scotland with the help of charismatic evangelist John Knox who preached the more fundamental views of Calvin to establish the Presbyterian Church in 1592.
- ✓ In Sweden, Denmark, Norway, Finland and Iceland the less brutal views of Luther were adopted earlier starting in 1527.
- ✓ In the Netherlands, then ruled by the Spanish under the umbrella of the Holy Roman Empire, the north part converted to Lutheranism which in 1568 sparked a series of European wars culminating in the 30 years war(1638-1668) between the new European Protestants and the traditional Roman Catholics.

England seperates from the Roman Catholic Church and there follows a blood bath

In England the story went as follows:

Henry 8th with the support of Thomas Cromwell, (not to be confused with Oliver C) destroys Roman Papal authority in England. (1529-36) Note there was no theological change. Henry divorces Catholic Catherine of Aragon and marries his already pregnant second wife Anne Boleyn. Divorce not permitted under Roman Catholicism. Henry no longer has to pay taxes to the Pope and can keep the money for himself.

Henry kills Thomas Cromwell because he arranges a marriage to an ugly woman poor Anne of Cleves(from Catholic Flanders in northern France) and appoints Protestant convert Thomas Cramner as Archbishop of Canterbury. The Bible is translated into English for the first time and is distributed more widely thanks to the first printing presses in England which were housed in the Palace of Westminster (Houses of Parliament) to enable the King to keep control.

Henry 8th dies and his only surviving son Edward 6th is appointed King at the age of 10. Edward is advised by his uncle and more importantly Thomas Cramner. Edward is persuaded to convert to the ideas of Luther and became the first Protestant King. John Knox who later converted Scotland to the more fundamental Protestantism of Calvin works as chaplain to Edward 6th under Cramner.

Edward dies at the age of 14 in 1553 and is succeeded by Mary the daughter of Henry 8th and his first wife the Catholic Catherine from the Spanish Royal family. Not surprisingly Mary took England back to the Catholic faith under control from Rome.

Mary kills Thomas Cramner and in all about 300 newly converted Protestants by the then normal punishment for heretics by burning alive at the stake! She was nicknamed Bloody Mary. Mary marries King Philip, of Spain as the most powerful Catholic ally in the world. (Head of the Holy Roman Empire) but Philip leaves her.

When Mary dies in 1558 of cancer she is succeeded by a charismatic single minded and very intelligent Elizabeth the daughter of Henry 8th second wife the English girl Anne Boleyn. Elizabeth saw it was her duty to return England back to the new Protestant faith. Elizabeth was as ruthless as her elder sister Mary.

Elizabeth died after a reign of 35 years, no husband, no simple Protestant succession. James the 6th King of Scotland won the English throne in 1603 by virtue of his great grand mother being the daughter of Henry 7th . (And unified England , Scotland and Ireland). It was only in 1592 that Scotland had been converted to Calvinist Protestantism by John Knox. Powerful Catholic

Christianity

Englishman Robert Catesby visited James in Scotland when it was known he was to become King of England and thought he had persuaded him to take England back to the Roman Church. He was mistaken, shaken and horrified and vowed revenge. He hired a staunch Catholic freedom fighter (terrorist!) who had become an expert in explosives as a Religious mercenary in Europe. His name is now well known, Guy Fawkes.

A team of 12 set about blowing up King James and all his ministers at the next state opening of Parliament when they would all be under one roof in the Palace of Westminster now the Houses of Parliament. With all the Gun Powder in place in the cellar, the 12 took on a 13th to fund them for a few more weeks. He betrayed them and Fawkes, Catesby and their band were captured on the, you've guessed it, 5th November 1603. (All children in England remember this day with an annual firework party.) The Church of England has remained independent of the Papal rules from Rome ever since.

250 years ago

For 100 years after Protestant King James 1st (1603-1625) the English were fearful of the chaos which might occur if any King changed the faith of the country. James ruled over a not very Protestant Church of England, a residual but illegal Catholic following and a noisy group of Calvinist fundamentalists called the Puritans. The English Kings were trying to rule in Calvinist Presbyterian Scotland and an Ireland who refused to change from their sincere Roman Catholic beliefs. Not an obvious recipe for a quiet life for either King, the church or parliament.

1642 The English civil war. Religious background

Charles the 1st tried to rule without parliament, indeed he did not call his ministers together for 17 years!

Eventually he needed money to finance an army to quell various Catholic riots in England and particularly also Ireland. The Scots were also a problem as they refused to adopt the English Prayer Book. (All Calvinist religions ban any formal approach to prayer as is laid down in a Prayer Book and a heavy hierarchy including Bishops) Parliament refused the money as his ministers were frightened of what would happen to them if the King had a powerful army at his disposal. The King needed to be stopped and the way to do it was for the ministers to form their own army. Hence the Civil War.

Oliver Cromwell lead the Parliamentarians who were nicknamed "Round Heads" after the appearance of their metal helmets and their ultra short hair. The Kings army were nicknamed Cavaliers and retained the fashionable long hair of the time. Cromwell organised his army very well and spent time teaching them the art of battle and indeed formed a formidable fighting force. They won.

Cromwell did not become King but "Lord Protector" and quickly set about quelling the religious riots in England, Ireland and Scotland. He earned a reputation for being particularly brutal fully supported by his "Model Army". His excuse for wholesale human genocide was to cleanse his territories of religious dissidents for once and all. In both England and Ireland he was particularly hard on Catholics who he murdered in the name of God. Worse, in Ireland he kicked out any suspect landowners and replaced them with "good" Protestants from England. This mass ethnic cleansing was "successful" in six Irish counties. (Act of Settlement 1652). In Scotland he was reluctant to fight as Puritans and Presbyterians were both Calvinists, but the Scots refused to negotiate. So in went Cromwell and his Model Army. They won there too.

However the Protestant succession could not be guaranteed.

- ✓ James 1st 1603-1625 had only just been converted from being a Catholic when he became King. Surprisingly he ruled as a Protestant (Anglo Catholic) and not a Scottish Presbyterian Calvinist. He hated the English Calvinist Puritans to such an extent that many fled to America in 1620 (The story of the May Flower and the origin of Thanks Giving day in the US)

- ✓ Charles 1st 1625-1649 had left all religious matters to his Archbishop Laud a ruthless Protestant Cromwell 1651-1658 was a ruthless Calvinist Puritan but preached religious tolerance! This is supported by the fact that he re-allowed Jews back in the country after an absence of some 400 years.

- ✓ Charles 2nd 1660-1685 although he had been in exile in Catholic France and was married to Catherine of Braganza a Catholic from Portugal, when offered the English throne he ruled as a Protestant. Parliament was very much ruling the country and were very nervous of the threat of the Puritans to the extent of passing the following Laws (Clarendon Codes):-

    - ✓ All Clergymen and people in local government must take (Protestant) Anglican communion.
    - ✓ Those not attending Anglican Sunday worship would be punished.
    - ✓ Puritan and any other non conformist meetings (including Catholic) to be limited to a maximum of five people.

Charles on his death bed "converted" to the Catholic faith which would rather indicate he had been a

Christianity

Catholic all along only admitting to it to improve his chances of getting to heaven by receiving the last rites from a Catholic priest.

Charles had no children by his Catholic Portuguese wife but having many mistresses he had 14 illegitimate sons and daughters.

- ✓ James 2nd 1685-1688 was the younger son of Charles 1st who during the reign of Charles 2nd had shown great leadership in charge of a huge expansion of the English Navy but was a Catholic. He promised parliament he would supress any desire to bring England back to Catholicism but no, from 1688 he tried to introduce a "Declaration of Indulgence" that was a cancelling of all laws against Catholics and the other banned religions.

    Parliament's response to this alarming change of

heart was to send a message to the husband of James' daughter Mary, the Dutch Protestant Prince William of Orange, and asked if he would like to send an army to England and claim the throne for himself. (Mary had refused to accept the crown unless also offered to her husband). When William arrived in London James fled to Catholic France and Parliament had the Protestant king they wanted. This was not the end of the matter however. James went to Ireland with an army of French mercenaries where he knew he could gather more loyal Catholics to form a huge army to get his throne back.

Their first job was to eliminate any Protestant support in the north of Ireland. They lay siege to the town of Derry (or Londonderry) where the Irish Protestants had fled, confronted by such a formidable army. The new English King, William of Orange came to the rescue, the siege was lifted and James and his Catholic army regrouped south by the river Boyne. Protestant William routed the Catholic army of James who fled back to France. This victorious battle of the Boyne is celebrated by the Irish Protestants (Ulster Orange Men) annually to this day. On the death of William his wife's Protestant sister Anne inherited the throne

- ✓ Queen Anne 1702-1714 married Prince George of Denmark and they had 17 children but they all died! Hence a protestant successor had to be found once more.

- ✓ George 1st 1714-1727 was the best they could find, a German King (King of Hanover one of the states of the Holy Roman Empire) and great grandson of James 1st. German George spoke no English (he communicated with his Parliamentary ministers when he had to in French). Initially he surrounded himself with German advisers but latterly appointed a chief English Minister, Robert Walpole. England has had a chief minister or Prime Minister ever since. George had very little to do with running the country setting the example for all future Kings and Queens thus eliminating the problems brought about by the religion of the Monarch.

The Enlightenment

The so called Enlightenment occurred during the same period described above i.e. about 250 years ago. As the name suggests thinking people became "enlightened" at this time by the first real forays into science, a renewed interest in philosophy, human rights and freedom of speech. Up to this time any criticism of the Church or the King could be a reason for execution. Science brought about ideas which were contrary to the stories in the bible and the teachings of the Church.

Frenchman Voltaire's words summed it up: "I may disagree with what you say but I will defend to the death your right to say it"(Circa 1750) The official end of the Enlightenment was the French Revolution (1790; people versus the King) but in religious terms the end was some 50 years later with the publication of "The origins of Man" (Englishman Darwin in 1859 and 1871). Darwin postulated the theory of development of animals and humans by natural selection or survival of the fittest.

This flew right in the face of the "Creation" in the bible and made Christians wonder what other parts of the teachings of the bible and the church should be treated with a pinch of salt. Church teachers to this day are struggling to come to terms with the findings of modern science. The difference in the last few years (perhaps 25) is that Voltaire's wish for a free and open debate is now possible in England and to a lesser extent most countries in the western Christian world.

The main contributors to this revolution for freedom of speech and the arguments to debate were:

- ✓ Rene Descartes 1596-1650 Frenchman. Worked mainly in Scandinavia as it was too dangerous for him in France. Noted for:
  - ✓ Theology Roman Catholic
  - ✓ Mathematics, Geometry
  - ✓ Philosophy, There are two things in the world, mind and matter. Quote "I think therefor I am".
- ✓ John Lock 1632-1704 Englishman. Philosopher and writer. Noted for
  - ✓ Human rights
  - ✓ Kings have no "divine" right to rule.
  - ✓ Human ideas come from experiences, Humans are born with a blank mind.

- ✓ Blain Pascal, Frenchman, Physicist and Philosopher. Noted for:
  - ✓ Mathematics
  - ✓ Fluid mechanics
  - ✓ Mechanical Calculators
  - ✓ Theology
- ✓ Sir Isaac Newton, 1642-1727 Englishman and Jew. Professor at Cambridge. Probably the most famous and influential of this period. Noted for:
  - ✓ Understanding gravitation. Looking at apples falling off trees to the earth and seeing this is the same force as causes the moon to orbit the earth. Hence completing the maths started by the Italian priest Galileo who was nearly burnt at the stake some 200 years earlier by proving to the Pope that the Earth orbited the sun rather than the other way round as expounded by

the church. The Popes took some 500 years to admit the church was wrong.

- ✓ Mathematics, invented calculus.
- ✓ Optics, discovered that white light (sun light) is made up from 7 primary colours.
- ✓ Calculated the age of the earth as 3500 BC. (Some way out as we know now but he used the biblical texts)

✓ Francois Voltaire, 1694-1778 Life long campaign against injustice and intolerance. Spent time imprisoned in the famous Paris jail, the Bastille. Released and fled to England. He ended his life in Switzerland. Noted:

- ✓ Philosopher and moralist.
- ✓ Scientist
- ✓ Writer, campaigning for human rights in Religion and Politics.

Christianity

A few years later we had the Darwin family. Grandfather Erasmus Darwin 1731-1802 Medical science, and his most famous Grand son;

- ✓ Charles Darwin 1809-1882. Charles postulations were so revolutionary that at first he dare not publish them. Following a study of animals he proposed that the "Creation" in the Bible was wrong and that animals were not created as we see them now by God but that they evolved into what they are now through a process of "natural selection" or survival of the fittest. Most noted for:
    - ✓ Medicine
    - ✓ Biology
    - ✓ Religion

After Darwin the attitude of most Protestant Christians was never the same again. The majority felt that many doctrines needed to be continuously updated to take into account the advances in Science, particularly Medical Science. But at the same time the basic teachings of Jesus were still valid for example: "Thou shalt not kill" and "Do unto others as you would they would do unto you". Roman Catholics who need to have the nod from the Pope before their religion can embrace a change generally take many years longer to permit new ways. Good examples in Medical science are: Abortion (of an unborn child, understandably the most controversial) , Contraception and the genetic creation of human organs for saving the life of fellow men.

Still 250 years ago

An explosion in the varieties of Christian expression
Indeed going back 500 years to the reformation, there were many reformers each producing a different version of the Protestant faith. The earlier reformers were of course Englishman Wycliffe followed, Luther

and Calvin both active more than 500 years ago. In England the Church theology adopted, mainly under the guide lines of Archbishop

Thomas Cramner, are not strictly Protestant. The Church of England is best described as Anglo Catholic. If it were Protestant the religious hierarchy would be much flatter and Bishops would not exist on the basis that humans in such a powerful position can corrupt the Church. The Church of England retains a similar hierarchy to the Catholic Church but the head of the Church is not the Pope but the King or Queen of England.

The other main difference is that changes can be made much more easily in the C of E as the effective leader is the Archbishop of Canterbury who is much closer to the needs of his flock than can ever be possible when the head of a church is remote and speaking for a large number of different countries. Thus true followers of

Luther and Calvin could not follow the path of the C of E and a huge variety of Protestant Churches have been formed, mainly in England, as follows: (In date order)

- ✓ 1530 Lutheranism. Followers of Luther of course, the original and now the biggest Protestant Church worldwide. (80m followers) The official church of the Scandinavian countries and much of Germany also strong in the US. The Church was reluctantly accepted by the Holy Roman Empire following meetings in Augsburg in south west Germany in 1530 Charles 5th present and 1555 Ferdinand 1st present. Lutheranism as such has churches in England but other Protestant churches are much larger.

- ✓ 1560 Presbyterian, Started in Scotland by John Knox who was a Calvinist. Hence Presbyterians have no Bishops or prayer book and no religious Icons like pictures of Jesus and no Alter in

Church. Became the official church of Scotland in 1696. Also many Presbyterians in the North of Ireland.

- ✓ 1570 Puritans, started in England in the reign of Elizabeth 1st by those who thought the C of E was too Catholic both in management i.e. the retention of Bishops, and in "Popish" rituals like wedding rings, taking one's hat off in church and the retention of Icons. These English Puritans expected James from Presbyterian Scotland to become a Puritan but he persecuted them instead. Many then fled to America to form a new colony. (The Mayflower/Thanksgiving story)

- ✓ 1640 Quakers originally the Society of Friends. Some of the Puritans who remained in England formed a new sect under George Fox. They were noted for a distinctive dress (very simple), hard work, pacifism and Puritan worship. They were also persecuted and in 1682 in the reign of Charles 2nd under their leader William Penn they followed their friends the Puritans to America. (King Charles 2nd gave the area in America now called Pennsylvania to Penn as a Quaker sanctuary)

- ✓ 1750 Methodists. Followers of John Wesley. Again a back to basics Protestant Church which split from the C of E in 1790. Now the largest Protestant faith in the USA. Simple theology; repentance, faith, love. The Wesley family wrote many hymns regularly sung in English churches to this day.

- ✓ 1872 Jehovah's Witnesses. Founder American Charles Russell. Not a Christian religion but followers see Jesus as their sole prophet/leader (but not the son of God) and hence will not take orders from secular leaders. Always pacifists. Originally called Watch Tower Bible and Tract

Society. One of the most active door to door evangelist movements in England.

✓ 1879 The church of Christian Scientists opened in Boston USA for followers of American Mary Baker Eddy. 1821-1910. Mary was a sickly child but was much improved by the faith healer Phineas Parkhurst Quimby. Devotees shun any modern medicine and rely solely on prayer and meditation for cures. There have been many cases of Christian Scientists dying unnecessarily having refused medical treatment in hospitals. A very popular movement in England in the early 1900s.

✓ 1950 New Age is one of the latest religions initially created by English girl Alice Bayley when living in the USA. The movement gathered momentum following six events:

- ✓ The Beatles interest in Indian religions particularly Hindu and their enthusiastic following of Transcendental Meditation as taught to them by the Hindu guru Maharishi Mahesh Yogi
- ✓ The American musical "Hair"
- ✓ The Vietnam War.
- ✓ The assassination of President Kennedy.
- ✓ The 1960s sex revolution
- ✓ The conversion and preaching and the books of film star Shirley MacLaine

Followers believe in reincarnation, are quite often anti western culture and look for a new "truth" and way of life.

Humanists

In summary we can compare the beliefs of the Secular Humanist with those of Christianity. The idea of humanism did not start yesterday but 700 years ago as science began to demonstrate that all the teachings in the bible could not be taken as gospel. During the Renaissance the movement gathered a pace but early humanists still believed there was a God. Dutchman Desiderius Erasmus (1466-1536) perhaps the most influential humanist thinker of the Renaissance period was invited to England by Henry 7th and influenced Henry 8th. The movement further gathered strength during the Enlightenment and has retained a strong following ever since.

Comparing modern Humanists with Christianity we have:

All Christians believe there is a God.(Bible Genesis Ch. 1)	Humanists are atheists that is they say there is non God.
Christians believe that humans, following the sins of Adam and Eve are born evil and need to repent to God	Humanists believe all humans are born good and it is up to individuals whether they

by following the teachings of Jesus before they can be considered good.(Genesis Ch. 3)	choose good or evil.
Humanists believe man discovers truth and wisdom through logical thought	Christians believe all truth is Gods truth and all discoveries are only part of what God has created.(Acts of the Apostles Ch. 17 v. 24-28)
Humanists believe morals are developed by human experience and debate which can include the teachings of Jesus or any other secular or religious moralist.	Christians believe that morals and ethics must be based on Gods written word (Bible Exodus Ch. 21) and the teachings of Jesus (Bible Saint John Ch. 1)

Christianity in England Today

All Christian faiths are now free to worship and there are many more Roman Catholics than might be expected in a Protestant country. This is mainly due to a million Catholics coming to England at the time of the

Irish potato famine 150 years ago. The Queen is still head of the Church of England which is clearly a problem in a country which has so many other accepted faiths. This is sure to be debated in depth over the next few years. Church attendance is very low at below 5% of the population and the Christian churches have no visible recruiting programmes. The emphasis is how to live side by side with followers of other faiths.

Early British Christianity

The history of early British Christianity has long been recognised as a subject of wide importance. Even in the seventh century its facts and fictions had power to affect religious beliefs, to decide the choice between rival churches; and those facts and fictions have still their weight. The answers to the historical problems when and how Christianity grew up in Britain still influence practical conduct, and, in such a case, one may be pardoned for trying, now and again, to restate the truth as gradually revealed by research.

The following paragraphs contain an attempt to summarise what is now certain or probable respecting

Christianity

British Christianity during the first four centuries of our era that is, during the Roman occupation of our island. The task is difficult. We do not know much of Roman Britain, and the little which we do know has never been collected into any satisfactory whole; the student has no general conspectus to aid his judgment of details, and more or less mischievous misconceptions are not unnaturally very common. This state of things increases the need of such an attempt as I propose to make, but it also increases its difficulty and renders certain defects in treatment all but inevitable.

During the first three centuries we hear and know very little of Christianity in Britain. One or two passages in Tertullian and Origen may suggest that it was introduced at the beginning of the third century, though the rhetorical colouring of these passages forbids precise conclusions.

The full growth of the British church p418 in the fourth century is additional testimony to its existence in the third century, but we know nothing of its origin. We may conjecture, from the silence of ancient writers, that Christianity reached Britain by natural expansion rather than by conscious missionary effort. We may conjecture further from geography that this expansion was Gaulish or German, from the Roman provinces of Gaul and Germany that is, from what is now France, Belgium, and most of the Rhine valley.

The communication between Britain and Gaul was easy and abundant, that between Britain and Roman Germany was hardly less so. In the second and third centuries we find the armies of Britain and the Rhine exchanging recruits; in the fourth century, as Ammianus (18.2) tells us, the British corn ships were accustomed to sail up the Rhine. When or whence Christianity reached Gaul we do not know, but Otto Hirschfeld may be right in thinking that it came from the East to Marseilles and the Rhône valley and was established in Lyons not long before 150 A.D.

Arguing from these premises, we may state the following hypothetical origin for British Christianity: that during the third century (and perhaps earlier) individual Christians on individual errands reached Britain, most of them from Roman Gaul and Germany some, perhaps, from other parts of the empire, for the freedom of movement was very great and that thus gradually congregations were formed and in time bishoprics established, presumably by the aid of Gallican bishops. But this origin must be recognised as hypothetical: Christianity in Britain, like the university life of later England, sprang from a source which we cannot adequately trace.

This uncertainty has naturally provoked ecclesiastical historians. No less than six apostles have been supposed to have preached in Britain, and the suppositions, so far from being patriotic inventions of Englishmen, are due mainly to continental writers of the sixth and four following centuries; they are all, of course, guesses unsupported by any sort of evidence. In the seventh century a p419 more astonishing story appears. Lucius, king of Britain, we read, sent to Pope Eleutherius (about A.D. 174-189) and requested conversion: whether his request was granted, is not stated. The story is certainly untrue: it is wholly irreconcilable with general history and is rejected by historians of all creeds and schools by Duchesne, Stubbs, Mommsen but its history is worth sketching. It appears first in the biographical list of popes known as the 'Liber Pontificalis,' and in such a way that we may be sure it was inserted in that list at some time before A.D. 700. From the 'Liber Pontifical is' it was copied inaccurately into the 'Historia Brittonum,' often ascribed to Nennius, and more accurately into Bede's 'Ecclesiastical History;' thence it has spread abroad, and it is still occasionally quoted by ignorant or unscrupulous controversialists. Its origin can hardly be doubtful. Through the seventh century, from Augustine's landing in 597 to the Whitby conference in 664 and Aldhelm's letter to Geraint in 704, a violent controversy raged between the British and Roman bishops, and the arguments used on both sides for instance, at Whitby were largely historical. Religious controversies have in all ages been fertile in conscious or unconscious forgeries; the appearance of the Lucius legend at Rome, at the end of the Romano-British dispute, may well be due to that dispute itself. Such an invention need not disturb our conclusions as to British Christianity in the second and third centuries.

With the fourth century we find a fully grown British church. The Diocletianic persecution of A.D. 304 reached Britain, though not, perhaps, in its full fury, and later ages ascribed to it the martyrdom of Alban of Verulamium. In 314 three British bishops from York,

London, and Lincoln Eborius de civitate Eboracensi, Restitutus de civitate Londinensi, and Adelfius de civitate colonia Londinensium (probably an error for Lindensium) with a presbyter, p420 Sacerdos, and a deacon, Arminius, attended the council of Arles, in the south of Gaul, and British bishops were present, if not at Nicaea (325) and at Sardica (343), yet certainly at Ariminum (359).

Bede refers to churches at Canterbury built during the rule of the Romans to which I shall return later on. Near the end of the century Victricius of Rouen came over to mediate in a dispute, doubtless about ecclesiastical matters. Our other literary references to Christianity in fourth-century Britain are vague and plainly prompted by the fact that Britain, the remotest west of the empire, was suited to rhetorical antitheses. By the end of the century it is able to produce men like Pelagius the heretic, and Faustus, abbot of Lérins in 434 and bishop of Riez in 461. Early in the fifth century

Christianity

(A.D. 429) the British church was visited by Lupus and Germanus; and perhaps about the same time Fastidius Priscus, Britannorum episcopus, wrote his tract on the Christian life. It is plain that by 400 or 420 Christianity had made vast progress in Britain.

To our literary proofs we may add much archaeological evidence, hitherto somewhat neglected. 1. The Christian monogram and formulae have been found in many parts of Britain. The Cherish-Rho occurs in three villas. At Frampton, in Dorsetshire, it has been set (as it seems) into a fourth-century mosaic, adorned with a head of Neptune and some verses relating thereto; at Chedworth, just north of Cirencester, it has been cut on four building stones; at Harpole, in Northamptonshire, it seems to occur in a pavement. It occurs, further, on many small objects on a silver cup found at Corbridge, near Hadrian's Wall; on two silver rings from the Roman villa at Fifehead Neville, in Dorsetshire; on a bronze object from York; on a tin vessel from the south, and occasionally on lamps. The formula Vivas in Deo occurs on gold rings from the fortress at Brancaster and the town of Silchester; and the Thames near Battersea has yielded, at different times, no less than eight similar blocks of pewter (tin and lead) stamped with the name Syagrius, the Cherish-Rho, and either the words Spes in Deo or the letters A-Ω. The name Syagrius first appears prominently in the fourth century, and to that date we may assign the blocks found in the Thames.

2. Inscriptions in stone are scarcer. None has yet been found in Britain which can be certainly ascribed to a fourth-century p423 Christian, and few which can plausibly be so ascribed. The phrase plus minus, however, which is often used of a man's length of life on Christian tombstones abroad, appears on the fourth-century tombstone of Flavius Antigonus Papias, recently dug up at Carlisle, and on one (or two) tombstones found at Brougham, in Cumberland.

Christianity

Inscriptions contribute also three curious pieces of negative evidence respecting the growth of Christianity, which deserve attention, although two of them are perhaps only probable. (i) The most important of the three is comprised in an inscription found recently at Cirencester. A square 'basis' or pedestal is inscribed on three panels (the fourth is lost),

That is, L. Septimius, governor of Britannia Prima, restored a column and figure of Jupiter, which had been erected by older piety and had fallen into ruin. The original column and figure was probably set up about A.D. 150-250: the restoration, beyond question, dates from the fourth century, and there can be little doubt that it is due to some pagan revival, perhaps that of Julian, called the Apostate. The spread of Christianity had caused the monument to fall into ruin: some governor, zealous for the 'old faith,' restored it

The inscription does not bear on it such obvious marks of date as its Cirencester fellow, but it was (we are told) found with coins of Carausius beneath it, and it has all the marks of being a restoration at the end of the third or beginning of the fourth century. The reason for the ruin is not stated clearly: the words per insolentiam dirutum suggest, however, the explanation which I offer. (iii) The third piece of evidence is provided by the tolerably numerous class of altars erected Deo Veteri or Dibus Viteribus⁰ which occur in the north of England.

These altars are small, rudely cut, and often illegible, and belong obviously to a late date; they seem to indicate a worship of the 'old gods' the prisca religio of Septimius at Cirencester. It is noteworthy that they have been p424 found mainly or wholly in military posts, where (as we should infer from other evidence) the old religion lingered latest. This evidence of inscriptions two or three doubtful tombstones and a few negative records may seem a small matter; but it is really considerable.

In many parts of the empire the custom of erecting inscriptions decayed during the fourth century: in Britain that custom was never vigorous, and at the period in question it stopped almost wholly. A few milestone, a military inscription from the Yorkshire coast, and those which have just been mentioned form almost the whole record. Christianity clearly plays a prominent part in our fourth-century epigraphy.

3. Inscriptions do not exhaust our evidence; there are definite remains also of at least one Romano-British church. In 1892 the excavations at Silchester, the Calleva Atrebatum of the Romans, resulted in the discovery of a small building which by its ground plan declared itself to be a fourth-century Christian church. It stood or stands east and west. The central portion is thirty feet long and ten feet wide, with a western apse;

on either side are aisles five feet wide; at the east end is a porch, or narthex, seven feet deep, extending the whole width of the building. The 'nave' was floored with coarse red-tile tesserae, but in the apse is a panel, five feet square, of finer mosaic work, marking probably the position of the altar. Outside the building eastwards is a small tiled erection, perhaps the cantharus, and traces of a courtyard, perhaps the atrium.

The resemblance of the whole to the fourth-century churches discovered in Italy, Africa, Syria is very striking, and, though the first announcement of the discovery was greeted with natural scepticism, there can be little doubt that it is a Christian church. I may allude here to another early church, the famous St. Martin's at Canterbury. The definite testimony of Bede (H. E. I.26) asserts that this church was originally built in Romano-British days, dum Romani incolerent Brittaniam that is, certainly before A.D. 445 and recent examination has convinced some good judges that the nave of the present structure is Roman work. More probably, however, the church, as it stands, dates in its oldest portions from very early Saxon times.

The preceding paragraphs have summarised the literary and archaeological evidence which we possess concerning fourth-century Christianity in Britain; it remains to deduce the character of the British church from this evidence. It was a fully organised church, with three or more bishops; it numbered adherents in all parts of the Roman province. The seats of the bishoprics were in three of the largest towns. In Britain, as throughout the western empire, Christianity spread first and fastest in the great centres of city life.

It was not, however, confined to the largest towns; we have detected its traces both in the smaller towns and in the villas of southern and central England. How large a proportion of the population accepted it we do not know. The toleration shown by Constantius Chlorus, the direct protection shown by Constantine doubtless favoured its spread in Britain and Gaul at the end of the third century, and the evidence quoted above shows that at least in the latter half of the next century Christians must have been in a majority in some parts of Britain.

On the other hand one class seems wholly uninfluenced. We have no clear sign of Christianity in the army. In the great legionary fortresses of Isca (Caerleon) and Deva (Chester), in the huge military frontier which extended from the Humber to Hadrian's Wall, the presence of the new religion is almost imperceptible. In this Britain resembles the rest of the empire. The imperial army, recruited from peasants and barbarians, pagani and gentiles, contained few Christians. Diocletian and Licinius were able to exclude them from military service without sensibly lessening the supply of men.

Fifty years later Julian (A.D. 360-363) wrote with much satisfaction that 'the mass of his army worshipped the gods.' Some of this adherence to the old religion is visible not only in the rank and file, but in the officers and the official class generally. We know the names of few fourth-century officials in Britain, but it is perhaps not an accident that the praeses L. Septimius appears at Cirencester as worshipping Jupiter, and that Magnus Maximus, p428 who enjoyed high military command in Britain from 368 to 383, was converted only in 382. After the death of Julian Christianity perhaps spread faster in the army; but this cannot have affected Britain. In 383 Maximus struck a blow for empire and took across the Channel the larger part of the Roman forces. For the next thirty years the Roman government in Britain was weak and intermittent; by degrees it was wholly abandoned.

If the view here indicated of British Christianity be correct, it follows that another view, lately put forward with some confidence, is wholly inaccurate. It has been argued by Mr. Hugh Williams, in a paper read in 1894 before the Cymmrodorion Society, that the church of fourth-century Britain was 'the church of the resident Roman population, not of the people of Britain.' According to this view the only Christians in fourth-century Britain were Romans, and on their 'final departure,' in 410, the existing church collapsed.

Instead a new church arose, the church of the Celts; in 410 they had been mostly heathen, by 450 they were mostly Christian. In support of this opinion Mr. Williams urges four considerations. (1) He emphasises the military character of Roman Britain. Roman civilisation, he says, was a varnish which disappeared from the legions. (2) He cites the names of the British clergy present at Arles as the names of Romans. (3) He brings forward parallels from Gaul; and (4) he notices the absence from Welsh literature or tradition of any reference to fourth-century Christianity. I shall venture a few criticisms on this view.

In the first place Mr. Williams seems to me wholly to overrate the Celtic element in Roman and post-Roman Britain. He does not stand alone in this. It is the present fashion to call the Roman occupation an interlude, after which an unaltered Celtic civilisation resumed its interrupted supremacy. This view is the natural outcome of the most recent political developments; it is naturally dear to Welshmen, and a scholar is perhaps foolish to protest against it. Nevertheless it is quite unhistorical.

It is quite true that Roman Britain was a military district. As a frontier province it was strongly garrisoned, and its garrison must always have formed its prominent feature. At first, perhaps, this garrison was the only important thing in the island; but that was not the case in the fourth century. The 'departure of the Romans' in 410 was not a departure of foreign officials and troops taking with them a foreign civilisation. It did not mean what the departure of the French from Algeria or the English from India would mean to-day. Roman civilisation spread widely during the Roman occupation of our island, and it lasted one if not two centuries after their final departure. In the fifth century the towns of Britain were inhabited as in the fourth, and were known by the same names.

The Britons largely used Roman nomenclature and spoke the Roman tongue. They tilled their fields, probably, on a Roman system of agriculture; they retained parts of the Roman military system, and about 470 A.D. they sent 12,000 men to aid the Romans against the Visigoths in Gaul. Even in the sixth century they called themselves Romani in contrast to the surrounding barbarians. This Roman civilisation was perhaps limited to the nobles, clergy, and better educated persons, and it was naturally not permanent;

communication with Rome ceased, while neighbouring Celtic influences encouraged Celtic ways and speech. But there were really romanised Britons; they are not imaginary persons, as Mr. Williams seems to think. And from their ranks came the five British clergy at Arles, only one of whom bears a British name.

In the second place Mr. Williams's view seems to me in direct opposition to the comparatively abundant evidence on the subject which I have mentioned above. Mr. Williams confines his fourth-century Christianity to the actual Romans in Britain. But the facts show that the specially Roman elements of the army and officials were not specially Christian; whatever Christianity existed would be unaffected by their departure.

On the other hand this Christianity can be traced in many places where Roman influences were not specially present, in towns like Silchester and

Canterbury, which we are accustomed to call Romano-British rather than Roman, and in villas. It seems clear that it was a Romano-British Christianity, such as would not be dependent on the presence of Roman officials and would survive the end of the Roman government. There is, therefore, no need to assume (with Mr. Williams) a general and spontaneous movement resulting in a new and popular Celtic church. We have no evidence of such a movement; we have not even time for it. Mr. Williams allows it thirty years, but the result is too vast for one generation to produce. Mr. Williams's theory has been invented to explain an imaginary difficulty, and it has no proofs to support it. It is doubtful whether it ought to have been put forward.

p430 The truth appears to be that the church which existed in fourth-century Britain continued without interval or interruption into the following centuries. Changes, of course, came with time. The visit of

Christianity

Germanus in 429, the growth of monasticism, the gradual preponderance of the Celtic element among the Britons, the gradual retreat on Cornwall, Wales, Cumberland, the conversion of Ireland these and other such facts could not fail to influence British Christianity. But the changes were not changes in kind.

The British church which argues with Augustine in 597, with Wilfrid in 664, argues in defence of things which many western Christians must have thought obsolete in the seventh century; it was, perhaps, a more conservative church than those which had come to be united as the church of Rome. We have no reason to doubt the essential continuity of the church in Britain from its foundation somewhere in the dim days of the second or third century till its entry into the full light of medieval history

www.ingramcontent.com/pod-product-compliance
Lightning Source LLC
Chambersburg PA
CBHW021113080526
44587CB00010B/507